RAPID RELEASE

How to
write & publish *fast*
for profit

JEWEL ALLEN

Rapid Release
Copyright © 2019 Jewel Allen
Cover and interior design: Jewel Allen
First publication: January 2019

Special thanks to the following: My beta readers and author friends for the valuable feedback. My sprinting friends, without whose smack talk I might not have been able to finish the entire burrito. As always, my husband and children for your love and patience and not taking me too much to task for dirty bathrooms. Last but not the least, my Heavenly Father for giving me the opportunity to write.

Thanks to the following authors who graciously shared their advice on rapid releasing, either on social media or in response to my request.

Bree Livingston
Sally Britton
Jo Noelle
Eliza Boyd
Brittney Mulliner
Brian Meeks
Audrey Rich
Lacy Andersen

Lucy Roberts
Kristen Iten
Chandelle LaVaun
Yumoyori Wilson
Angel Lawson
Iris Kelly
Julia Keanini

For updates and publishing news,
subscribe to my newsletter

www.JewelAllen.com/subscribe

Table of Contents

Chapter 1: Why this book?

It was the spring of 2018. I had been self-publishing novels since 2014 and my sales had tapered to an average of $11 a month on my 11-book backlist. I just wanted to finally make some real money on my writing.

I paid roughly $600 per book towards covers and editing and ended upside down for months. I had already warned my husband that I may have to dip into the family savings as things stood, and he looked unenthused. I needed to try something new.

A few weeks later, I attended a *Breaking Amazon's Top 100* writer's retreat and took away two key pieces of advice: 1) write a series in a hot market and 2) release them rapidly (one a month).

In the following Book Report graphic, this was how the year 2018 went for me. Can you tell when I started rapid releasing?

I made $2,210.59 that first full month on my first book with the second one on pre-order. The taller spikes are Kindle Unlimited page reads and the smaller ones are sales. I made this income with hardly any advertising and mainly by swapping newsletter space with other clean romance authors. I hadn't a clue what I was doing.

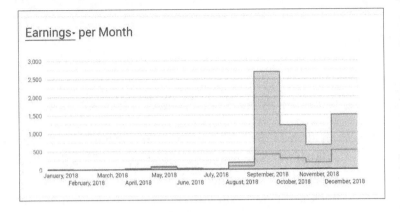

Earnings· per Month

As I've networked with other authors to cross-promote my books, I discovered that although many are already rapid releasing, there isn't a lot of literature out there showing how to do it.

Thus, I wanted to write a book that could help other authors by showing the actual steps I took to rapid release a series profitably over a five-month period.

Here are some caveats:

- My novels are clean contemporary romance. Though the principles should be applicable to other books, the results might vary slightly for other genres. I do devote a chapter to writing clean romance for those who want to learn what works for the genre.

- All my kids left for college about the same time I started rapid releasing, so aside from my responsibilities serving on the City Council, I write full-time.

- Rapid releasing will require some initial investment towards covers and editing, and a supportive family or spouse.
- Rapid releasing will *not* help you produce quality books unless you are willing to study the craft and practice, practice, practice. If you have never really written a novel, you will want to read some how-to writing books. And write.
- This book won't teach you everything about marketing and launching a book into the stratosphere, though I might touch on those points. It can, however, get you well on your way to having profitable books.

I can guarantee, however, that I will teach you everything I know about how I rapid released a profitable series. I will show you free to inexpensive tweaks that can help you make a profit right away. I will also show you how I rebooted my process as an author, improved my sales and bottom line, and helped breathe new life into my publishing career.

Ready? Buckle up and let's go!

NOTES

_____
_____
_____
_____
_____
_____
_____
_____
_____
_____
_____
_____
_____
_____
_____
_____
_____
_____
_____
_____
_____
_____
_____
_____
_____
_____
_____
_____

Chapter 2 : My Publishing Journey

Before I was a self-published author, I was a journalist and memoir ghostwriter. In October of 2014, to much fanfare and expense (I had Filipino food catered and my mother brought roasted pig), I launched my first novel, *Ghost Moon Night*.

The next few years, I followed up *Ghost Moon Night* with books in a variety of genres. Young adult. Zombie. Historical. Non-fiction. Romantic mystery. None of them to market.

In early 2018, I looked at my author checking account. I had spent more than I had made from publishing books that were not written to market. I knew I couldn't continue publishing without dipping into family funds.

I had to do something different.

NOTES

Chapter 3: What triggered the change

I was sitting in the *Breaking Amazon Top 100* retreat venue in sunny St. George, Utah, when I got the epiphany: *tweak your book ideas and incorporate them into a to-market series you can Rapid Release.*

This was not a new concept for me. I'd heard this several times before. My mind and heart must have been more receptive than usual, though, thanks to the retreat.

At the end of that day, I returned to the condo where I was staying, a fire lit under me. As though I was on the verge of something great.

For one, I was determined to try a different method. Whereas I had written what I wanted before without much thought to how it would hit the market, I was deliberately thinking of my book before I put a single word to paper.

I decided I would write a clean billionaire romance series. I felt a little twinge of apprehension since I hadn't even read one before, but I pushed my anxiety aside. I came up with a half-dozen titles, the first one of which was *My Billionaire Bodyguard*.

I'd already had an idea before for a story with a country superstar having a second-chance romance with her ex. I could set the story in Nashville, TN, which I had been to, so I wouldn't have to research much. Why not use that idea and spin it into a clean billionaire romance? I needed to outline it.

Once I started typing, I couldn't stop. Two hours later, I had a seven-page outline for this first book. I was excited. I couldn't stop thinking of my characters and plot, even through the next workshop day.

I went home from the retreat, expecting my session takeaways to amount to nothing. That first night back, however, I decided to make a cover for the first book.

I wasn't super great at cover design, but as an amateur photographer, I had a good eye for what looked good, and I came up with something sufficient. I left it up on my computer to inspire me and so I could imagine the male MC (main character). I finished book one's outline and researched Nashville further. I also looked up the MC's occupation (bodyguard). I then went on to tackle an integral part of rapid releasing, writing fast in a popular genre.

Ready to dive into specifics? Let's go!

NOTES

Chapter 4: Choose a Popular Genre

Before June of 2018, never in a million years did I think I would be writing a billionaire romance, let alone rapid releasing a series. However, I realized if I was to make money at self-publishing, I should at least be open to this.

***

Recognize Trends and Hot Markets

I am a member of several author groups on Facebook. Invariably, someone will ask, what do you foresee will be a publishing trend that one could write to market to? And that, my friend, is the billion-dollar question.

Remember after *Twilight* came out and vampires were the hottest thing? Or when *Fifty Shades of Grey* came out and billionaire romances boomed? Thing is, were they really trends, or just a new manifestation of a time-tested trope? Readers have always liked the wealthy, brooding Alpha male, who sweeps the heroine off her feet and makes all her dreams come true.

As I have embarked on my journey writing a billionaire romance series, people ask in these forums if the billionaire craze will eventually die down. I don't know the answer, but meanwhile, write to market. If you don't, some other enterprising author will, so it might as well be you.

So what if six months from now, the hot trend wanes? At least you are capitalizing on it while it's hot. That's the beauty of indie publishing, you can respond to trends much quicker than a traditional publishing process will allow.

***

How I chose what genre to jump into

- I paid attention to who was ranking high and studied their books. A vast majority were billionaire romances.
- I googled bestselling billionaire romances and noticed that they were mostly erotica. Which meant that for every twenty erotic titles, I could write a corresponding clean title. The sky was the limit!
- I joined groups led by authors who are making money from clean billionaire romance.
- And then I plunged in.

***

Embrace the trend positively

If I made a buck over every eye roll I get when I mention "billionaire romance," I'd be a billionaire by now. Well, okay, maybe not *that* many people are rolling their eyes. But I sure haven't met as much direct condescension or veiled derision from others, even for say, my zombie novels. I tried to let it roll off my back at first, but eventually, it got the better of me.

I tried to find my tribe on Facebook, but there were no clean billionaire romance groups. So I started the Facebook groups **Clean Billionaire Romance** (for readers and authors) and **Clean Billionaire Romance-Authors Only**. I wanted to create a safe place to aspire, to dream up billionaire scenarios and to exult over our successes without anyone judging. It's been fun gathering with like-minded individuals.

If I were to hazard a guess as to why there's a bit of pushback about billionaire romances, it's that the genre is so "in your face." There's so much of them they are starting to come out of readers' ears. Usually with the photo of an attractive Alpha male, with promises of far-fetched plotlines.

Which are the same things that attract readers to the genre.

By the way, the billionaire trope, or common literary device, has been around for ages. Wealthy man sweeps heroine off her feet; sound familiar?

So whether you want to try your hand at billionaire, cowboy, royal or regency romance, or whatever hot trend/market/trope you want to try, find others who share your interest, read well-reviewed books, and embrace your chosen genre wholeheartedly.

One caveat: if you find it hard to get excited about your potential genre, perhaps you should consider another one. Readers will be able to tell if you're less than enthused about it. Plus, you won't have fun writing those books.

***

Write what you love and tweak it to what is trending

In 2018, one of my author friends tweaked her already published series so that the main character was a billionaire. After she changed the cover and title, she got an orange #1 bestselling flag. I wanted to earn the same kind of money and get the same ranking as her, so I tried to replicate what she did.

When I finally sat down to brainstorm a series for rapid release, I thought of how much I love writing romantic suspense and mystery. I knew that by itself, that genre might not sell as well as others. Why not meld that with a hot genre like billionaire?

Going through my list of book ideas, I settled on the story of a country singer who hires her billionaire ex to be her bodyguard on her Nashville tour. Bingo.

NOTES

Chapter 5: Think series

One of my takeaways from the *Breaking into Amazon's top 100* retreat was that series was the way to draw in the readers. After all, if they like your first, they will read the next and next and next.

As I envisioned my billionaire series, I wanted them to have a common thread, but be standalones. By the time I was writing the third book, some readers would say they wanted certain side characters to have their own love story. Whenever I could I obliged. That's how Katy starred in *Her Billionaire Santa* and why Thelma agreed to a fake engagement in *Her Billionaire Spy*.

I put in some sly cross-references. For example, most of my characters come from Sunnyridge, Colorado. So much so that my husband has said the fictional small town has an inordinately high number of billionaires. Someday, I aspire to have a big scene where all my billionaires could be reunited and interact.

TAKEAWAYS:

- You can formulate a series based on similar tropes, geographical area, profession, trope (billionaire, cowboy, royal).

- Link together standalone books into series. I had two books that were both cozy mysteries. I changed up some wording in the formatting, and voila, the books were tied in a series.

- Follow the rule of thirds. Write at least three in a series before starting another series. Your readers will have more confidence in you finishing a series and commit to reading your books.

NOTES

Chapter 6: Use catchy book ideas and titles

To choose the title, I researched on Amazon to see what titles were already taken. I initially titled this first book *My Billionaire Bodyguard*. After I got a suggestion from a writer's group, I changed it to *Her Billionaire Bodyguard*.

Book ideas are everywhere. Here are some origins for my stories.

I traveled the summer before college to a girlfriend's province. Her uncle's baby died and I watched the family's funeral procession on the beach. (*Ghost Moon Night*)

I wanted to write about an Irish billionaire but I didn't know if there was such a person. I googled Irish billionaires and found out that the youngest self-made billionaire was, indeed, Irish. (*Her Billionaire Valentine*)

One of my side characters in a novel kept referring to her charity work in Guatemala, so I spun off a Christmas novel set there. (*Her Billionaire Santa*)

I was buying ice cream at the store and saw a cowboy walk past. (*A Cowboy for Christmas*).

TAKEAWAYS

- Write down your titles and book ideas when you get them. Or you will forget.
- Check to make sure there aren't a billion books with the same title on Amazon, and if there are, at least be aware there might be some confusion later. P.S. Titles are not copyrightable, but I would steer clear of using titles like *Twilight* or *Harry Potter*. I imagine you might be sued for trademark infringement.
- Depending on your trope—billionaire, royal, or cowboy—put that word in the title, if possible. If not, add it to the subtitle. At the very least, put it in the blurb. Having that word in there will make it searchable.
- Test your titles on reader groups.
- If your title sounds clunky, it probably is.

NOTES

Chapter 7: Write the blurb and outline first

When I decided to start my clean billionaire romance series, I tried writing the blurb first. I wanted to make sure I had a viable series. Once I had a blurb for each book in the series, I went ahead and wrote an outline for book one.

Since I started rapid releasing, outlining has been an invaluable tool for me. If I start a story without outlining, it's okay for the first little bit, and then my plot runs out of steam. In the middle of the story, I'm throwing in all sorts of mayhem just to keep the story alive. Or type The End and have to backtrack with additional scenes.

Writing the blurb first can provide you a guide as you write your story. If you find yourself veering off-track, look at your blurb and make sure all of the main plot is working towards the story goal.

It doesn't have to be rigid, however. If you need to, adjust your blurb as your story grows.

***

How to write an effective book blurb

Many people dread writing their blurb. I used to pay a bestselling author forty five bucks per book to write my blurbs, that dreaded copy that goes in your Amazon description or the back of your print book. She would ask me to summarize the synopsis of my novel on two pages, double-spaced, and then I would wait for her to give me back a working blurb. After some back and forth, I would approve a final blurb.

In June 2018, I decided to try something different, and not just to save money. I not only started writing my own blurbs, but I did so before I started my story.

It's hard to quantify the effect of those blurbs on my sales, but the shortest blurb I came up with for my clean billionaire romance series generated me four figures the first full month out of the gate without advertising. There are so many factors that went into that, I'm sure, including the popularity of the genre, but if I had a lame-ish blurb, it very well could have dragged down my sales.

I have been thinking of what has changed for me since those days when I used to hire out my blurbs to now, where I actually enjoy writing them. There are many ways to skin a cat. This is how I've approached it:

- **Write out the blurb before I start the story.** If I couldn't distill my story in four or five lines,

I knew I had a plotting issue. It meant that the thrust of the story was too scattered. When I wrote out the blurb ahead of time, I not only had a high-concept blueprint for my story, I also already had a blurb right after I completed the story. Two birds with one stone! I have tweaked my blurb after I write a story, once I identify a theme.

- **Only I have a unique insight into my story.** When I hired out my blurbs, I was pleased with them because they sounded like a movie description you would see in an ad. Packed with punch with blockbuster potential. But something seemed missing, which wasn't the fault of my blurbist. It was missing the heart of the story. The uniqueness and the essence of why I even wanted to write the story in the first place.

- **Writing a blurb isn't as simple as filling in the blanks.** You know those fun madlib games—you put a noun here, an adjective there, and voila, you have a story. But that is a cookie-cutter approach that I believe prevents the author from tailoring their blurb to their story. Listen to your story. Listen to your heart.

- **The blurb must capture emotion and style more than fact.** Recently, I weighed in on a four-paragraph blurb on Facebook. It mentioned the location names, details about the characters' pasts, inner thoughts, fears, goals…it was simply too much. A blurb needs to get down to the essence of the story.

- **If it's a romance, you need to give one or two solid one-liners on the male and female characters.** Usually it has to do with the inciting incident that attracted them to or repelled them from the other person, what would be the main obstacle to their relationship, and a story question you need answered.

- **The shorter the better.** We are all busy. Our readers are all busy. As I have been sending out newsletters and swapping with other authors, I've had to analyze a lot of blurbs so I can cut due to space. My goal is to shorten them for my busy subscribers. In doing so, I discovered something interesting.

One book had too long of a blurb so I cut it out completely and used only the tagline. The next time I studied my stats, I was surprised to see it got the most clicks. Again, that could be the cover and the genre (royal romance), but despite the lack of details, readers were intrigued enough by it to click. Now, when I write a blurb, I try to keep it to about four sentences max for the characters and two lines at most for the story problem. I then look at the blurb again and strip it of any unnecessary words.

- **Don't bury the lead.** When I used to write news pieces, I put everything I wanted in the story right off in case the reader doesn't finish it, or the editor cuts it for space. Same with a blurb—you should put the important information early on to catch your reader's attention. Some blurbs warm up before getting to the meat of the story, meandering with backstory, word-building and interesting but random details. In the first sentence of your blurb, tell me about what motivates your MC.

- **A blurb is meant to entice, not to summarize everything.** Entice the reader to open the book to find out more about your characters. Why should they read the book when they can just read your blurb? Keep some mystery.

- **The blurb must match the style and feel of the book.** Is your book funny? Emotional? Scary? Suspenseful? Then your blurb should reflect that.

- **Avoid trigger words and TMI that make a reader uncomfortable.** I have seen blurbs that make me feel uncomfortable. If you ever come across one, listen to your gut and note why so that you avoid it in your own. This is one of those hard-to-quantify characteristics, but it reminds me of advice my college writing professor gave me. She said, choose your words with care. Some words just sound too...depressing. For a light and breezy romance, this is like the kiss of death. It's like going to a party and sitting beside someone who tells you about his problems from the get-go. You smile politely but move on in a hurry.

• **Pay attention to blurbs of bestselling books**. Study how they're constructed. You will see that there isn't a cookie-cutter answer to a great blurb. The best blurb is the one that works for your book.

• **Writing your blurb comes down to having confidence.** It means going with your gut as a storyteller. What stays, what goes. It's great to be humble and ask people for feedback on your blurb. I still do that occasionally. I ask people to weigh in on my blurbs on Facebook. Ultimately though, only you will know what your blurb should say.

• **Practice makes perfect.** The more you write your blurbs, the better you will get at it. Hire someone if you must, learn from their technique, then experiment on your own.

NOTES

Chapter 8: Mock-up the cover as you write

I have had my covers designed and I've designed my covers. As I have a hands-on background in marketing and graphic design, I can generally come up with good concepts for my covers. I use a free photo software, Gimp, which is a lot like Photoshop.

However, I am still lacking in photo manipulation skills. I have a good eye for which models convey the emotion I need conveyed, but I can't quite get the lighting right, and when I share my DIY covers in groups, invariably someone will say it looks photoshopped. So when I can, I try to hire someone to do my covers.

For *Her Billionaire Bodyguard*, I started out with a cover concept, just so that I could visualize my characters and write with them in mind. I liked to post the cover on my laptop desktop so I could be inspired to write.

If you'd prefer to not do a mock cover, you can also make a Pinterest board with the main characters, settings, and other things related to your book.

NOTES

Chapter 9: Hire a cover artist

After I finished the manuscript of my first clean billionaire romance, I finalized the cover. My first attempt had a handsome but glowering man in a suit. I ran my DIY version past fellow authors, most of whom did not like him.

With that feedback, I picked a cheerier couple who looked in love and added a purplish concert background. I tried to do it myself, once again with unsatisfactory results. I ended up hiring a cover designer to convert my concept into reality.

My artist not only did so with the proper lighting, but she also designed the title and branded my series. It was one of the best business decisions I've ever made. Once I decided on my series and had the designer make my first one, I commissioned her to make four more.

This is one area where you can still have a good product with a reasonable cost. My e-book covers cost me less than $100. You do not need to shell out hundreds of dollars on your cover. Save this money and increase your profit margin.

Check out *Her Billionaire Bodyguard*'s Before (man) and After (couple) covers. Note the improvement in font and branding.

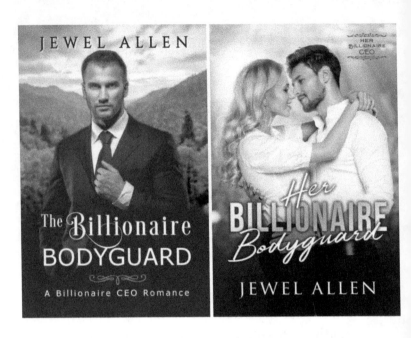

NOTES

Chapter 10: Commission series covers at once

For my *Her Billionaire CEO* series, I commissioned my artist to make five book covers all at once.

Some advantages were: a) I got a series discount (be sure to check with your designer if this is an option) and b) I didn't have to wait to get my cover designed when the book was ready. Especially since I did pre-orders, it was handy that my covers were already done. I was able to put my next cover in the series on the last page of my latest release. My first book got 69 pre-orders as a result.

The disadvantages were: a) I had to plan my books well ahead of time or at least had to know the general gist of it and b) Once, I decided the current cover didn't fit my protagonists, so my artist had to re-do that one, costing me more.

Most artists are fairly inexpensive nowadays. Since the cover can make or break your book, I highly recommend that you hire someone to make a professional cover that hits the genre expectations.

You can find artists on Fiverr, though I must say in my limited experience, they have been less than stellar, where I didn't get what I thought I was paying for. I got my money back the second time this happened, but it left a sour taste in my mouth for that site.

I have hired artists before for $35 for a basic cover to $300 for a more complex one. Pre-made covers are also an option. Those usually can run anywhere from $30 to $150. Some can go for lots more money.

The one drawback to the pre-made cover is that if you want to do a series, you are pretty much committing to that artist. Check their prices and make sure you can live with those rates for a future book. Otherwise, it's an economical way to go.

Chapter 11: Believe that you can

When I started rapid releasing, I often asked myself if I could truly publish one book a month. After all, it takes me 30 days to write a 50k-word novel during National Novel Writing Month in November.

Despite my trepidation, I plunged on.

Maybe it was sheer naivete. I didn't really know what I was getting myself into. I didn't think that editing and revising would take up quite a bit of time which I needed to build in for each book.

Setting a pre-order date month to month certainly was the whip that drove me to reach my publishing goal. It was an unforgiving whip, but without a deadline, I firmly believe it would be easy to let my publishing goals skitter by the wayside.

Before rapid releasing, my only other pre-order experience was with my first novel, *Ghost Moon Night*. I wanted to have it ready for a Halloween release. As the deadline got closer, I realized I was going to run out of time to get my book ready. Thankfully, an author friend helped me edit the manuscript round-the-clock so that I could put it out in time. We pulled all-nighters, sending my document back and forth. I managed to meet my deadline, but it was such a nerve-wracking experience, I vowed never to do it again.

That was four years ago. I have gotten more publishing experience since. Eventually, I taught myself how to format my e-books and print books. I wrote manuscripts quicker and learned the mechanics of romance writing.

Doing a rapid release schedule is not for the faint-hearted. Especially when you haven't stockpiled manuscripts ahead of time. (Read Chapter 16, "Alternative to writing month to month" for more information about stockpiling books ahead of time as well as joining multi-author groups.)

There have been moments, leading up to my pre-order deadline, when I've had a panic attack, unable to breathe easily, my heart pounding like crazy. I just had to tuck my head down, grit my teeth and power through whatever needed to be done.

As you finish every project, your confidence will grow. Mine did, after the first two books, when I recognized they weren't just flukes. I could possibly duplicate, triplicate the process.

A couple of years ago, an author friend of mine pumped out novellas like crazy. She shared publicly that some of her friends had talked to her about it, sharing their concerns that she would be hurting her brand with her fast output, and maybe even impacting other authors. At that time, I watched in awe as she talked about producing book after book.

I didn't think I would ever be able to do what she was doing. Now I have.

Speaking of having faith in yourself, let's talk in more detail about pre-orders.

NOTES

Chapter 12: Enroll your book as a pre-order (optional)

A pre-order is an option for e-books on Amazon and other outlets where an author can put their book up on sale a maximum of 90 days before its official launch date. It is a free option and could be a good way to encourage series read-through. For example, at the end of book one, you could put the cover and link to the next book so that your reader can buy it.

I like to put mine up every 24th day of the month. There is a lockout period three days before your deadline when you cannot change the file. Be sure to upload your manuscript before that deadline, and pay attention to what time zone conversion it is. I once tried to sneak in before that deadline and realized it was Greenwich Mean Time. I missed the deadline and had to ask Amazon to push the right file to my pre-order buyers. It was possible, but the hugest pain and could possibly alienate your readers.

I like having deadlines, so pre-orders work for me. It encourages me to be productive. I also like to be able to give out the link to my book ahead of time to authors I'm swapping newsletters with.

I use my last published book's file as a placeholder file as the manuscript and then switch it out with the correct one before my pre-order deadline. It helps that I aim to write 50k-words per book, so the file size pretty much stays the same when I change it out.

If you choose to do pre-orders, you are better off setting your pre-order deadline as far out as you can especially if you've never done this before. If you cancel or delay your deadline you could lose your privileges for a year.

Pre-orders are not for everyone. I did it for my first book and I wasn't ready for such a stressful deadline. I made it, but it was harrowing. I swore it off the next four years but decided I could try it this time, having had a few more books under my belt.

It might also depend on what kind of books you write. I write contemporary romance which requires minimal research. If I were writing historical, I would need to take more time.

Build in some family, sick and vacation time so that you are not working yourself to the bone to meet this deadline. Schedule your pre-order deadline week so you have open days to do your revisions. I usually take a full week to incorporate my editor's suggestions, and that is working on it around the clock with occasional breaks for other responsibilities and open evenings with family.

NOTES

Chapter 13: My 50k words in 5 days Experiment

From June 26-30, 2018, I wrote a 50,000-word novel in 5 days. *Her Billionaire Bodyguard* is now published. Below is the play-by-play of how I did it. If you want an alternative to writing this fast or writing a book a month, check out Chapter 16, "An Alternative to Writing Month to Month."

Day 1

My youngest left for a week-long girls' camp at 8:30 a.m. My veterinarian husband was at work. I had the house pretty much to myself. I watered my container plants outside and got everything I needed to sprint. My laptop, water bottle, calculator, phone and charger.

Sprinting is writing as fast as you can within a time limit, anywhere from 15-30 minutes. Some people do it against themselves. I like to sprint with other writers in Facebook groups dedicated to this writing method. Google Writing Sprints and you will find some good ones with authors serious about getting a lot of words down fast. I will touch more upon sprinting in Chapter 15, "Write in Sprints."

My goal was to get 5,000 words towards this new book. I was a fast typist, but usually during National Novel Writing Month, I struggled to get 1,300 words a day in 30 days. I wrote all morning and reached my 5k goal. I discovered why an outline was a good idea. I could just write each scene and not have to pause to think about the plot.

I took a break for lunch and then decided to join sprints in the afternoon and again late at night to see if I could get more. I got 8,263 words total. Not bad. I went to bed at 12:25 a.m.

Day 2

I vacuumed the house before anything else. Having been gone on the retreat and since I am not fond of housekeeping, I had shirked my duty. After a 7:30 a.m. fitness class so I could look good for author photos, I went through my chores like the Tasmanian Devil. With a clean house (and conscience), I went into my office and sprinted 8,494 words. On my Facebook page, I predicted, "At this rate, I can finish this book in seven days."

Day 3

Ten o'clock that next day and I already had 4,100 words under my belt. The words piled up but my story was getting out of hand. I didn't have a good grip on character motivations and the romance obstacles were getting a little over-the-top. I decided to take a break for a bit, re-outline, and then work some more.

In the afternoon, I sprinted with some high word-count sprinters who write 900-1,000 words in 20 minutes. They made me feel like a slow poke but it opened my mind to possibilities. I decided, hey, I can see if I can do that. And it turned out I could!

It was a revelation to realize I could physically write this much by (a) constantly typing and (b) having a scene that I could flesh out for 1,000 words in twenty minutes. I could have just sprinted by myself, but the pressure of sprinting against others doubled and tripled my productivity. For one thing, I couldn't slack nor navel gaze, add/subtract words, waste my time of Facebook, etc.

At first, I wanted to see how much I could write above 8k. And then 9k. And finally, I was so close to 12k so I pushed for that before midnight. Just to see what I am physically and mentally capable of.

That was how I spent most of my day, sprinting from about eight to ten in the morning, then again from two until eleven, with a break for dinner, walking the dog, and helping my hubby with some chores in the yard. My days were usually not as open as they had been those three days. All that writing time had been a gift. The process of speed-creating was exhilarating.

That same night, I reached a milestone. I wrote the most words I'd ever written in one day, 12,270. To give you perspective of how that broke down, during a 20-minute sprint, I could usually produce

500-700 words. My output meant I sprinted roughly 20 times, which translated to six hours of white-heat writing.

I finished the day thinking that I wanted to seize the momentum and get more words that Friday and Saturday. Maybe even finish the book. Which hadn't even really occurred to me until I was trying to do it.

Day 4

I went to fitness class first thing, showered, and then went to work on my manuscript. By two p.m., I had written 5,217 words. I was itching to do more, but I went to help my mom pack her kitchen for a remodel, and later, helped a neighbor move.

Starting at ten p.m., I wrote another 3,079 words for a day total of 8,296. Which brought my manuscript to 39,358 words of a 50k goal.

I re-outlined again, so I could figure out how many sprints could produce the chapters I need. That was about twelve more scenes. I was flying by the seat of my pants. There was stuff I hadn't researched ahead of time, but I decided to just write it and research later.

I went to bed wondering if I could crank out 10,642 words the following day to finish the first draft. Suddenly, the prospect of getting 50k words in 5 days seemed viable.

Day 5

By midday, I reached my wordcount goal with 5,216 words. I reached another personal record — during a 20-minute sprint, I was able to write 1,043 words. Typically, I would get 700, with a bit of hemming and hawing. I was sprinting with a couple of fast sprinters and I couldn't afford to pause. Nothing like some friendly competition to get the fingers flying. At 43,000 words, I already reached the ending and could have called the story good. But I really wanted to get 50k.

At 3 p.m., my family and I spent the afternoon and evening with our daughter at college. We ate out and hiked. By 9 p.m., we headed home. I wrote about 2k words in the car. We got home at 11:30 p.m. and I still had 5k words to finish. By the time I went to bed, I crossed 50k.

NOTES

Chapter 14: Prepare to write fast

To summarize, these were the steps I took *before* I even tried to write a 50,000-word novel in 5 days. I followed these steps for the first book of a to-market series, but the tips can apply for a non-series book as well.

- **Plot a to-market series and how this book fits in it.** My goal was to have a viable quality draft quickly so I could have it start making money for me soon.

- **Write a short, catchy blurb that reflects the tone of your book and gets to the heart of your story.** Re-read this often to keep your draft on track. If you can't come up with a three-sentence blurb, your plot is too vague and your draft will most likely have plotting issues.

- **Make sure you are excited about it.** If you aren't excited about the book, it'll be hard to get motivated to write. And you will be writing a lot. The advantage of fast writing is hopefully you won't get bored with your story. Plus, if you get ideas for other books, you know you will be able to get to them quickly after this one.

- **Make a mock or actual cover.** This is optional, but to me, this was a very helpful step. (I do this for all my books.) Looking at the picture of my MC inspired me. As exhaustion set in, looking at my cover kept me going.

- **Write a detailed outline.** Tweak it so that the story makes sense, but do not obsess. It does not need to be perfect, and even the best-laid outline will need to be flexible. Include key scenes and even dialogue, if they come to you already. These keystones will prime the pump.

I have been a pantster, too. Which can be fun. But it is going to be tough to write a 50k-word draft in five days that will not require major revisions without some sort of a plan or direction. I've been there done that. Though I finally published those projects, I had to practically gut them and start over at the revision stage. Not fun nor was it easy.

NOTES

Chapter 15: Write in Sprints

For me, sprinting has been the key to writing fast. Most days, I try to keep my schedule clear for sprinting with other authors in Facebook groups. I love sprinting on Scrivener, though lately, I've enjoyed sprinting on Word.

Someone calls the sprint. We go for 20 or 30 minutes, and type (hopefully without distractions) and then compare word counts at the end of the session.

I love sprinting. It gets my competitive nature going, and I usually pour out the words hoping I could beat my fellow sprinters. If nothing else, it forces me to keep my fingers flying, to not check Facebook or my stats or my email or anything else that could distract me. Another advantage is that I am not thinking too much about what I am writing, not letting my brain talk me out of putting down the words that I tell myself is drivel.

If I am not sprinting, my word count production descends to about a third of what I am capable of producing against other people.

Here are some sprinting tips:

- **Sprint with others.** The competition and accountability will force you to write. Arrange it ahead of time with your family that they shouldn't disturb you while you are sprinting. I just say, "I'm sprinting," and they know they can talk to me in 20 minutes. If you can't sprint with others, sprint and time yourself. Fast-writing by yourself is a skill you can train yourself to do over time.

- **Figure out character names and setting details ahead so you don't have to waste time as you write.** Keep track of new characters on a master list. If you can't remember or figure out a name, just write "whats-his-bucket" or a generic "the maid."

- **If your outline goes haywire, take a deep breath and just keep writing.** You're a writer, make something up! You might just stumble upon a great plot point or character reveal. If you need to do more research, just make a placeholder note and keep going. Between sprints, re-outline if needed. For me, putting short phrases in caps in my Scrivener scenes reminds me of what happens next and which chapters still need words.

- **Speaking of Scrivener, use the Project Targets to give you a visual of where you**

are sitting on your wordcount overall, daily, and scene goals. There are probably other programs out there that can accomplish this, but I've really liked Scrivener. Learn more about the program at www.literatureandlatte.com/scrivener.

- **Add scenes that can lead to substantial writing in terms of character development, action or setting.** It's harder to keep the words flowing if you are jumping from short scene to short scene.

- **Sprint first thing or the soonest you can during the day.** Set a daily word count goal and stick to it. Break it up to morning and afternoon goals. Be ambitious while recognizing your limitations. This will allow you to still have a life and balance. After morning sprints, take care of your family, your job, etc., then get back to more sprinting.

- **Pick a week when you can get lots of writing time.** Luckily, when I wrote *Her Billionaire Bodyguard*, my youngest was at girls' camp and the hubby was at work. If you have other scheduling obligations, clear a block of time so you don't have interruptions to your writing.

- **Pray about it.** Express gratitude in prayer. The universe will in turn bless you in abundance.

- **Record your wordcounts every time you sprint.** I put mine in a note on my phone. Soon, you will see a pattern of how many words you could produce in 15 minutes, 20 minutes, etc. It's motivating to see the numbers add up. I make a game of seeing if I could break my record. The numbers will also let you know what wordcount you still need. If your goal is to write a novel in five days, divide up your overall wordcount goal by five and do it. Believe you can.

- **Determine your best writing time and write then.** I discovered that after lunch, I was too sleepy. Mornings and evenings were my best time.

- **Get up and take physical breaks as much as you can but don't allow for too long of breaks.** Seize your story's momentum while your head is still in the zone.

- **Schedule time for exercise.** I try to exercise three mornings a week, for an hour. Writing requires stamina, and this will give you energy. It can be something as simple as brisk walking, climbing stairs, gardening, etc.

- **Stay off FB unless you are sprinting on an FB group.** Even so, minimize the screen to avoid getting distracted.

- **To stay alert, snack on sugar-free gum.** Nuts and trail mix are also good options.

- **Sprint without music.** I find that without music, I immerse myself in my fictional world easier.

- **Friendly competition is good, but keep everything in perspective.** Just because someone can sprint a lot of words doesn't necessarily mean there is something wrong with you. Their words might even need to be revised a ton later.

- **Don't get down on yourself, if someone's output is higher than yours.** Continue to be supportive of faster sprinters as you'd appreciate the support. As long as you are putting down the words, that is progress.

I have written slow before, I have written fast. Overall, I think the quality of my work is better with fast writing. The story flows better and I don't have lag times where I forget what my book is about.

Plus, the draft is done before I am bored with it and I can move on to revising.

***

Writing fast doesn't necessarily result in poor quality

I thought for sure that the quality of my writing would suffer. After all, I was churning out my stories as fast as I could. Contrary to this, my sales have not only gone up, but my reviews have stayed high as well. I chalk that up to a few things.

First, as I have written more to-market romance, I am getting better at writing to genre expectations. Secondly, romance readers are discerning, voracious readers, but they don't expect as much nitpicky detail in a mystery or suspense subplot as a hard-core mystery fan. Some details that worried me seemed to not worry my readers looking for a light, escapist read. There will, of course be that extra-discerning reader, in which case you should make sure your story makes sense.

Writing fast seems counterintuitive to quality work, but it doesn't have to be. The storyline stays fresh in your mind. In the past, working on a manuscript over a period of months would require me to re-read my document because I had completely forgotten the storyline. The style was not consistent. I also got bored easily, because working on a story for months at a time felt tedious.

Writing fast can be a joy. I tend to write more in the cadence that I naturally speak or write, as my brain is keeping up with the torrent of words from my fingertips. Dialogue flies, especially banter. Writing fast also lends itself to humor. It's hard to write depressing plotlines when your fingers are flying on a drumming staccato.

I also love being able to get a story out there as quickly as I can.

For all the advantages of writing fast, I need to mention that writing and publishing fast can easily result in mistakes, crashing of technology at the last minute, and several other things brought on by exhaustion and a tight schedule.

One safety measure is to arrange editors ahead of time. A good editor is worth every penny. I alternate between two and they have saved me from scathing reviews. Well, at least they help keep them to a minimum.

***

Write to The End then go back.

I usually have great intentions starting a novel and outline pretty extensively until I get to the end chapters. At that point I tend to peter out.

I usually aim for 50,000 words which to some people is a "short" story, but technically speaking, I believe, is novel-length. Even after 16 books and counting under my belt, I still have a hard time getting to 50k. Despite my best-laid plans, I lose steam at about the 30k word point and start to slow down with my scenes. I do my best adding more words, and then zoom to the finish and usually a sweet epilogue.

Once that is done, I then go back and make a list of additional scenes, plugging them in to the right spot later. I have been able to increase my word count to 50,000 this way. For a couple of books, I have stopped at the low to mid-40,000s because I didn't want to add more fluff to the story.

Novellas (40k words or less) can be a good way to go if you prefer the shorter format. The advantage with novel-length in the long term is that your page reads will earn you more.

NOTES

Chapter 16: Alternatives to Writing Month to Month

To rapid release, you *do not* have to write a book month to month. In this section, four indie authors share their alternative methods.

***

Rapid Releasing a Regency Series every two months
by Sally Britton

Sally Britton is a sweet Regency romance author with six published titles plus two in pre-order (as of January 2019). In 2018, her debut year, she made $77,154 publishing a book every two months. Visit her at www.authorsallybritton.com

The first time I pushed "publish" on Amazon, I had no idea what I was doing. I really thought I knew, having done a few months of research beforehand, but I only had vague ideas of things like book magnets and why people sold books for 99 cents. There was a bit of a learning curve for me. I knew the best way to sell your book, the best advertising strategy, was to "publish another book." But it wasn't until after my first book was published that I learned about "slow release" and "quick release" methods.

Even after I learned about different release methods, none of them felt quite right for me and the way I write. I have a high output, I type quickly and cleanly, typically I can finish writing a book in six weeks. Those books are usually between 60-85 thousand words. I write historical romance, and I do a lot of research to help my books hit the market right. That being said, my goal has been quality of writing over quantity – because historical romance readers will rake you over the coals when you get details wrong!

Here are my publishing dates for my first year of writing in 2018:

The Social Tutor – January 30
Martha's Patience: A Novella – March 22
The Gentleman Physician – April 19
His Bluestocking Bride—June 6
The Earl and His Lady – August 1
Miss Devon's Choice – October 10

As you can see, I developed my own pattern pretty quickly. As soon as I figured out how useful magnet books were, I wrote a 17,000 word love story and got it on every newsletter builder I could. All my books are part of a series, but each can be read as a stand-alone. The magnet I describe as a "prequel," because it's about a couple already married in the first full-length novel.

I started doing my research in February, and I wrote my magnet and book two at the same time. I learned about people who published every two weeks or every month. I knew if I attempted that, my books would be shorter and feel less complete (for me) and that my historical quality might suffer. I had read enough indie-published historical novels to know that sub-par books in that genre might sell well initially but garnered horrible reviews. I wanted my books to be the same quality as those published traditionally. I found indie authors who wrote similarly to me and studied their release schedules. Many were about eight weeks apart.

"I can do that," I told myself. And I did.

The first month each of my books were published, I did newsletter swaps like a crazy person, but carefully planned. I shared three to four books a week in my newsletter, and I stacked shares with those authors to cover the first three weeks my books were released. Using my magnet, I grew my list to about 900 subscribers in three months (now most of my growth is organic and I'm at 15,000). I kept my content relevant to my market (sweet historical romance readers) and saw few unsubs. Swapping in that way kept my books purchased steadily enough to maintain a decent rank and keep showing up on other authors' "also-bought" list.

The month after a book was published, when I was knee-deep in writing or editing the next book, I would schedule features with affordable mailers like My Book Cave, Bargain Booksy, and E-reader

News Today, and lower one of my other books to 99 cents. I would also use my free days in the Kindle Unlimited program, one a month at least, on a Friday/Saturday a week before I launched the next book. I only shared those on social media and would ask other authors to share via Twitter or Facebook, too.

Something else I do to keep my books visible is run continuous Amazon Marketing Services (AMS) ads. It terrified me, at first, and I turned off and halted several ads when I wasn't certain what was going on with them. I set low budgets – sometimes only $2 a day. But as my sales grew, and I grew in confidence, I raised them higher and refined them. When my income grew, I budgeted more toward those ads.

Several of my books have hit the market just right, while I feel like one or two only get picked up after people read my most to-market books. That's okay with me. Read-through is an author's best friend.

I wanted to share all of this before sharing the data people most want – my income. Now, my numbers fluctuate, and I'm in a financial position where that's okay. We're a two-income household now that I'm writing books. I've experimented and seen rises and falls. Here are the numbers:

Jan: $30 (friends and family the day the book was published)

Feb: $189 (this is where I started learning, and I was focused on researching)

Mar: $167 (published my reader magnet and worked on growing my subscribers)

Apr: $525 (I was pretty thrilled – two books and a free magnet! Woo-hoo!)

May: $1,693 (no new books published, but started using ads)

Jun: $8,740 (third novel, fourth title, published halfway through the month)

Jul: $13,512 (did an author event and set a different book free ever weekend leading up to my next book)

Aug: $16,680 (my most to-market book was published and it has "bride" in the title)

Sep: $10,115

Oct: $12,490 (fifth novel, sixth title published, last book of the year)

Nov: $7,761

Dec: $5,252

A note about November and December. In 2018, for anyone not publishing a holiday book, this was a really difficult time to sell books. Authors previously making five figures made four, authors making four figures dropped down to three. We're still not entirely sure what happened. But given what all my other author friends were going through, I was amazed that I was still making a full-time paycheck with my royalties. I didn't do any advertising in November (still had a free weekend) but ran an international BookBub at the beginning of December. It didn't bump me up much, if at though I gained visibility in markets outside the US.

I'm off to a better start in 2019. I got a BookBub for a free book on January 1st and it's lifted me back into five figures. I have new releases planned for February and March, and I'm part of a popular anthology collection releasing in March, too. I have several books planned and I'm hoping to do even better than 2018's income.

My genre's fans are strict about what they expect in their books. The worst reviews I have are those that find fault in historical details I didn't write correctly (I go in and fix them when I find them). If I had to list my reasons for this much success during my first year of writing, it would be these and in this order:

- Polished, Professional Writing (Beta readers, critique groups, and an editor when possible.)
- Beautiful, Professional Covers (Your cover sells the first book, your writing sells the next one.)
- Established Author Network (I would be lost without authors in my genre supporting and sharing my work.)
- Advertising Within My Budget (Lots of options out there besides the $500 BookBub ad!)
- Advance Reader Copies (Build a review team. Each of my books launches with 15-30

reviews. Most are around the 100 mark now.)

You can do this. Experiment. Figure out what your readers, your genre expectations are and write with that in mind. If you can turn out books every few weeks, that's fantastic! If you need more time to prepare your product, that's okay too. Whatever you do, do it consistently and don't be afraid to be different. I'm shooting for every two months to either have something new or have a really amazing promotional event if I fall behind my schedule. One of my heroes in the indie world is S.K. Quinn. She had a book out that she's since retired all about publishing "For Love or Money." I've chosen to publish for both. I write what I love, but I'm smart about my marketing.

***

Rapid Releasing with Multi-Author Projects
by Jo Noelle

Jo Noelle is the pen name of a mother-daughter writing team. She writes dessert romances--satisfyingly sweet, and you'll want more. Visit her at **www.jonoelle.com**

We began working on a rapid release strategy with a multi-author group. First we built a world called Cowboys and Angels. Then each of the five authors wrote stories that would release two weeks apart. Each book was sequential to the previous ones. Although every story had a stand-alone happily-ever-after, the stories shared the location, characters, and timeline of the story. It felt like a rapid release to the readers because they always had something new to look forward to and created a steady income stream in the series, but the authors would put a new book into the series every ten weeks. It is a much slower writing schedule for the authors.

A second multi-author project we're involved with had a little different strategy. In the Twickenham Time Travel Romance series, again we created a world, but this time the authors shared one central character and a location, then wrote stand-alone stories within the world. The books were released every two weeks, so it still feels like a rapid release, hooking readers and keeping them with the series and primed for the next book.

In both groups, authors do their own editing, covers, and advertising. Since Cowboys and Angels has a long history with over thirty books out, we try to correlate free days for books to bring new readers into the sequence. In both groups, cover design was determined before the first book was release, and all authors have to use the same design to create recognition for brand marketing.

There are some challenges too. How many people would you like in a group? Keep in mind your members might have vastly differing opinions about writing, story building, using characters, how to collaborate, heat level of the romance, and entrepreneurial drive. Decide the parameters of the group before you start.

We've enjoyed some great benefits with multi-author project rapid releases. First, both of these strategies allow the authors time to work on other books and series not related to the projects. Second, authors "pool" their readers and maximize profits by capturing new customers they might not have had. Profits are dependent on how established the authors in the group are in the genre. Third, it helps build your base. Many fans from other authors have followed us to our other books as well. Fourth, there's no downtime for the readers to wait for another book, like there could be if an author has to write and save up books to be able to rapid release.

***

Rapid Releasing by Stockpiling Manuscripts
by Eliza Boyd

*Eliza Boyd is a sweet contemporary romance and women's fiction author who rapid released a clean billionaire romance every two weeks in January 2019. Visit her at **www.elizaboydwrites.com***

I'm doing Rapid Release right now. It's a great way to get a lot of books out quickly, build your backlist, and boost sales when a whole series is released in a close period of time (or the first three books). Plus, it puts three books in the "new releases" chart.

I wrote four of them, and they were ready before mid- December. I started writing in October. The first book took 8 days to write, the second took 10 (with 8 days of writing), the third took 9 (with 7 days of writing), and the fourth took 9 days. I let the first two sit until December and edited them in a week. I just finished editing the third one and I'll start editing the fourth one so I can send out ARCs early next week. And I'm releasing them all this month a week apart from each other. So the whole thing took 3-3.5 months because I was able to write them so quickly.

My stories are 40-47k words each, and I was averaging 5-6k, but the first couple of days are usually low word counts as I get into the story (even though I outline them, though I just started that with this project). So most days were 6k+ words.

I have no kids, no other job, just a husband who cooks dinner and encourages me to go after this dream. I'm really blessed. So I.gave it my all!

Now to figure out this marketing thing... LOL

***

Rapid Releasing a Sports Romance Series
by Brittney Mulliner

Brittney Mulliner is the author of a clean hockey romance   series.   Visit   her   at

<u>Planning</u>
1. Planned the genre and read a lot

As with any new story, I started by picking what genre I wanted to write and read A LOT of books. I wanted to make sure I understood reader expectations as well as finding a niche that I enjoyed that wasn't oversaturated. When I decided on Sports Romance, I knew I wanted to write hockey. It's a popular sport within the genre, but there wasn't a lot of Clean Romance so I knew that was an area I could target.

2. Picked tropes I like

Once I knew I wanted to write a hockey romance series, I needed to start planning the series story arch and each book. I gathered a list of tropes I like (forbidden romance, second chances, opposites attracts, etc.) Picking those out first helped me to develop the characters and plots.

3. Outlined a broad storyline for the series

Next, I decided how many books I wanted to write in the series. Since I wanted to write a series around one hockey team with the point of view changing for each book I could theoretically write an infinite number of books. I planned for five books, but as I got further in writing the series I've decided on six...or seven.

4. General ideas of how they meet and fall in love

Since I was planning a romance series, I outlined each book in a simple sentence of how they would meet and fall in love. This is what I had for two of my books:

LINE CHANGE (Employee/fake relationship) Colby Wells and Noah Malkin. He's new to the league and is in over his head. His agent hires an assistant for him and recommends they act as a couple to keep girls away.

ATTACKING ZONE (Enemy to lover) Kendall Davis and Wyatt Hartman. She's a die-hard fan of their rivals. She recently moved to the city but refuses to give up her hometown. They meet and she immediately knows who he is and puts salt in his coffee. (She's a barista.)

5. Studied successful covers and blurbs for the genre

Once I had a plan for my series, I did research on covers for the genre. I looked through Amazon's top selling charts for romance, clean romance, and sports romance. I wanted to make sure my cover would appeal to my audience, and clearly show the genre. I created a vision board of covers I liked then used that inspiration to design my covers. I repeated the same process for blurbs. I read over the blurbs for the top sellers and decided on a style I liked best, and worked for my audience.

<u>Execution</u>

1. Wrote three books before starting the publishing process for book one.

Everyone I talked to about rapid release recommended writing the entire series before releasing, but they were mostly talking about trilogies. I'm not patient, at all, and I knew I wouldn't be able to write all five or six books before releasing. I would explode from anticipation. So I compromised on writing three books before releasing book one. I was planning four week spacing so I figured I'd finish the rest of the series before book three was published so I'd remain ahead. Here are the publishing dates for the first five:

Jul 31
Aug 30 (4 ½ weeks)
Sep 27 (4 weeks)
Nov 8 (6 weeks)
Dec 18 (5 ½ weeks)

As you can see, writing #4, editing #3, publishing #2, and promoting #1 was tougher than I thought. My production time slowed down as things started piling up.

2. Built up newsletter

I used promotional sites to build up my newsletter over two years. This is something I'm not an expert on and constantly working on improving and growing my list. Your newsletter can be an invaluable asset so get to work on building that as soon as you can.

3. Planned NL swaps for each release

Don't have an advertising budget, newsletter swaps are your best method to spread the news about your books. Find a group (there are plenty on Facebook) that shares your genre and offer to exchange a spot in your newsletter with someone else. I've found that with my list a weekly NL is best and I swap with three authors each week. That's 12 authors a month sharing my book, all for free!

4. After book 5, I hit a wall.

Like I said before, production took its toll on me. After releasing book 5 I took a month off from everything, but marketing. I needed time to regroup and catch up on things. I felt horrible delaying things, but we're only human and the break helped me find my muse again and get back into things.

Recommendations

- Get more written before starting the release of book one!

The number one thing I would have changed is getting more books written before publishing book one. Or I would have had books 1-3 edited and ready for publication so I could focus on the next few books. I got too impatient and ended up burning out. Lesson learned.

- If you're writing to market make sure it's hungry.

I found in my research that there were not many clean sports romance so there was a risk of people not wanting it. Especially hockey. I later learned from other authors that most readers that read "hot and spicy" romance books will read clean but not the other way around. Fortunately, I've found an audience for my books, but I'd caution that if your goal is to sell books make sure your market is hungry!

- Make the titles and covers obvious it's a series

Make sure your series looks like a series. This will help the books sell each other. When you scroll through your genre you want people to see your books over and over again and make the connection that there's a whole series available.

- Preorders!

This is a controversial topic amongst authors, but I've found that pre-orders are successful for me. This is something that you'd have to try for your genre and see if works for you.

- Back matter in the back leading to the next book

I put the first chapter of the next book in the back of each with the preorder link so they can buy the next one as soon as their done. I don't want readers to forget about the series between releases so having a preorder available helps guarantee they'll keep reading.

- Be flexible. If you have outlines be flexible if characters change their mind.

I mentioned I planned for a five book series, but it's already evolved into six and possibly more. I allowed for additional books in the series by not having one hard ending. This might not be an option for some series, but I like the option of writing more or less than I planned. Characters sometimes have a mind of their own and may demand their own book or decide to difficult. Be flexible as the series grows and adapt to the changes.

NOTES

Chapter 17: Keep on moving

Often, publishing choices can be overwhelming. For example, after recently finishing a novel, I had a hard time deciding what to do next.

My next *Her Billionaire CEO* novel was due in two months. I got my custom covers for my next cowboy book. And I had an idea for this how-to book. This happened all at the same time. I couldn't decide which project to tackle. Especially since my brain felt foggy from exhaustion, having finished my last manuscript.

So I just started typing this book. I ended up drafting it in three days and revising it for another week.

If you are overwhelmed with choices, reach for the first project and keep on moving. Don't waste your time agonizing over which book to work on. As long as you are moving, you will be making progress.

NOTES

Chapter 18: You're not writing the Great American Novel

I aspire to write great books that readers will love and tell others about, but I have to remind myself every so often that my WIP (work in progress) is not the Great American Novel. I am writing escapist romances, and I am okay with that.

Whenever a scene feels mundane, I resist the temptation to change it up during the first fast draft. I figure that my editor will notice it and hopefully give me better suggestions. Unless I can come up with better alternatives to the wording, I just write my scene baldly, just to connect the dots. There will be time to polish it later.

This attitude helps me be more forgiving of my document, and less afraid that I am going to write something that will stink. Because I know it will until it gets edited.

When the voices in my head say that what I am writing is not worth publishing, about halfway through my manuscript, I just tune them out and tell myself I'm not writing the Great American Novel. If I am lucky, and the algorithm that floats bestsellers to the top works, then maybe one of these days I will also get that Great American Novel status.

NOTES

Chapter 19: Write through the dreaded middle slump

I usually know when I hit the middle slump in my fast drafting. My story drags, I am bored, I would rather eat caramel popcorn all day and get my fingers sticky instead of on the keyboard. I recognize the signs and it's scary because I usually have about 25k words that I just want to scrap and flush down the toilet.

This is what I do when that happens. I introduce a quirky character. In *Her Billionaire Spy*, I had her parents show up during her fake engagement. In *A Cowboy for Christmas*, I had her parents show up as well. Note to self: vary it up next time. In other stories, I usually introduce a funny side character, a conniving villain… anyone that can shake things up for both my protagonists and the world they live in.

Sometimes, the segue comes from nowhere and I have to adapt quickly to adjust my plotline. It gets hectic a little, but those characters breathe life into my story.

Whatever you do, step away for an hour, eat ice cream, don't give up on your story. Get past the middle slump and keep on writing until you get the word count you need.

If your plotline gets hijacked by a new subplot or character, do not edit and go back. Just keep writing as if Cousin Rita, Uncle Jack or Mr. Zoltack have been in your story this whole time. Make a note in caps to remind you to add them earlier in the story so they don't just show up like the proverbial "Divine Intervention."

If you are stuck on a part due to research or you can't quite describe something, keep writing. Even if it's placeholder words like, BLAH BLAH or PUT SOMETHING BRILLIANT HERE. Later you can go back and fill in the blanks.

The backspace key is not your friend. Resist the urge to delete words. You can delete them later just as well. You never know if you might need those words somewhere else. Deleting slows down your writing speed. Watch for the spelling and punctuation but don't obsess. You will catch them later.

NOTES

Chapter 20: Pay for professional editing

Your draft is done. Congratulations!

Should you pay for a professional editor? This is one of those areas that I think can vary from writer to writer. Some writers can write clean copy the first time around and more power to them.

Invariably, at an author's group, someone will ask, "Do you self-edit or do you pay for an editor?"

I think what the person wants to know is, "Can you get away with self-publishing without having to pay the hefty fee of an editor?"

I have done both with similar results, though I have a lot more confidence in publishing a book that has had professional editing. I don't recommend self-editing if you aren't confident in your writing, grammar and punctuation skills. Nothing will sink a book faster than a self-published book riddled with typos. You want to give your reader the best possible experience.

That said, the reality is, professional editing that is worth the money is expensive. The editors I hire usually charge between $400 to $600 for a 50k-word manuscript. That's a lot of money. If I weren't breaking even at least every month on my to-market books, I couldn't rapid release. Not unless my family can finance my books.

If you're losing more money than profiting, you need to take a good hard look at your genre, your audience, your covers, and your whole rapid release. I am not saying that all books have to make a profit right off, but it's not fun throwing money into a sink hole. You owe it to yourself and to your family to turn a profit on your books if you want to be able to sustain your publishing career in the long-term.

Due to the fast nature of rapid releasing, I am always looking for an editor who can give me my draft back quickly. I pay a bit more for an editor who can get me a thorough work-up on my manuscript and give it back to me in 72 hours. I love another editor who takes a little longer but gives me feedback with every revision so that by the time we are done with the process, I have a clean copy.

I know of a lot of authors who pay bargain basement prices on line editors. I did that once. Someone private messaged me and offered a deep discount on their editorial services. Anxious to save money, I paid this editor two hundred bucks. I didn't get much out of it other than catching a few typos and "This is great!" I learned the hard way that a) you usually get what you pay for and b) an editor worth their salt usually doesn't have to solicit authors for their services. They are usually booked months in advance.

Is it possible to not pay for an editor? I have done it with some books. Even then, I ask the help of beta readers, usually experienced authors, who can give me concrete feedback, whether in detail or big picture.

With one of my best reviewed and bestselling titles, I did not hire an editor. I did hire a professional beta reader for fifty dollars (yes, these people do exist, search on Facebook), who gave me helpful advice on plot holes and inconsistencies. It was a fairly clean manuscript. It just felt right, so I confidently published the book.

As much as I'd love that to be the norm, I haven't found that to be the case. I still pay between $400 to $600 for a good developmental and line edit for each book. Luckily, your investment will pay off in good reviews and a loyal readership.

Bottom line, make sure you can get other people's eyes on your manuscript, whether they be a professional editor, beta reader or professional beta reader.

OTHER TIPS:

- Before you give an ARC (Advance Review Copy) to your fans, get your manuscript to the best possible shape. One of my readers told me that because of the typos she caught in the ARC, she docked the book a star. Ouch. That hurts. Frankly on that book, I was past exhaustion and just put it out there. Not a good excuse, but it is certainly a reality. That is why a good line editor or betas can be gold.

- Read your manuscript out loud. You will be able to catch mistakes that way.
- Some authors do a gift card giveaway to readers who inform them about typos. I'm cheap, so I haven't done that yet. Make sure this does not go against Amazon's Terms of Service. It seems that if you are doing a prize for typos, you should be okay.
- Remember that no matter how much you scour a manuscript, there will be typos. Roll with the punches. If someone catches a typo and tells you, thank them profusely and update your file.

***

Book your editor in advance

Rapid release requires having all your ducks in a row. Good editors usually book months in advance. I have to contact mine at least two months out. We pick a date for me to submit my manuscript. One editor charges me before they start edits. Another one charges me after they make the edits. Whichever way you go, treat your editor well and they will treat you the same.

One of the best ways to find a good editor is to ask for recommendations from other authors. I send out a sample for them to edit. If I like it, I try out their editing for a month before committing to a long-term arrangement. I almost did that with my $200 editor, book several books at a time, and I am glad I didn't.

Usually when an editor private messages you with an offer, that should be a red flag. A great editor will be in demand and usually doesn't have to drum up business. The exception to this rule is an editor who is just starting out. They are great because not everyone wants a cut of their time and so they will have more time for you. Plus their rates will usually be cheaper.

NOTES

Chapter 21: Utilize beta readers

Beta readers are guardian angels in disguise. They are usually fellow authors or readers of your chosen genre who read your manuscript after you have done at least one pass through. If you haven't done that and you are giving someone a raw version of your book, that person would be called an Alpha reader.

Beta readers usually do this for free, or at least will trade manuscripts with you. They can be great allies in getting the best book possible into the world.

Over the past few years, as I have worked with betas, I have learned a few things:

- Decide if it is worth your time to trade manuscripts of similar length and genre with another author. You might save money by not having to pay someone, but you might also have to spend the next three days looking over their manuscript and giving meaningful feedback. There are professional beta readers who charge as little as $50. That said, they usually give only general feedback, definitely not line editing. That could be a great option for you if you want feedback right away with the assurance that someone can meet your deadline.

- Not all betas are created equal. Some will give detailed notes in the margins. Some will give you general comments. Either one is invaluable. Make sure before you arrange for a beta that your expectations are clear, to avoid hard feelings later.

- Make sure you are clear in what you will or will not beta. I am a member of a beta group who are members of my church. I assume that my standards are the same as theirs. As it happens, there have been a couple of times when I've been surprised by the content of their manuscripts and have had to abort my reading. It doesn't mean their manuscripts were bad, I just was not the right audience. Before you swap with someone, make your standards known.

Chapter 22: Format your book for free

Once your book is revised, it's time to format it for e-book or print.

As an indie author, I am always looking for ways to cut down on expenses as well as keeping control over the production of my books. When I accomplish both, hallelujah.

I used to outsource my book formatting, and they turned out beautiful books, but I didn't like having to ask someone to tweak my documents every time I wanted to change something or my links. Plus of course, I wanted to save money.

I love Scrivener for this purpose, but I recently had some formatting issues when I pulled my Word document into Scrivener. I'd heard you could format an e-book for free on Draft 2 Digital even if you are exclusive to Kindle Unlimited but hadn't actually tried it. I finally did, and it was amazing.

I did have to tweak some things to make sure the Table of Contents worked, but I'm sure over time it will be even easier. I love how easy it is to produce a mobi, e-pub or PDF of my document, and even include little graphics that make your e-book more interesting.

If you are new, it's okay to hire this part out. Since I started publishing in 2014, it seems like cost for this service has gone down. It is good to eventually learn how to do this for yourself though.

***

How to format a book for free on D2D

1. Set up a D2D account.
2. Click on My Books on right upper hand.
3. Add a book. It will take you to a details page. Upload the Word Doc.
4. Fill in the rest of the details info. Click save and continue.
5. Edit layout (add your cover and select how you want your Table of Contents to look like), then save and continue. I had to make my chapter headings, front and back matter headings larger in my Word doc so that the program could read them as Chapter headings.
6. It will take you to a preview page. Preview your doc and make sure it's as you like it. Play around with the template styles. Change your doc and reupload as needed.
7. DO NOT CLICK on the statement at the bottom left that says, "I have reviewed this manuscript and approve it for release to the sales channels I'll select on the following page."

8. Instead, click on DOWNLOAD mobi, epub and PDF buttons on the bottom right. Get your files and test them on your platforms. You should be able to use the PDF for your print book.

That's it. I don't do anything else and just log out. D2D saves my book as a draft so I can edit it as needed, and I have files that are ready to upload.

NOTES

Chapter 23 : Form an Advance Review Copy (ARC) team

When your book is ready to go out into the world, you can take an extra step and get your book to an Advance Review Copy team.

Some people call them scream team. Or fan club. I call mine Jewel Allen's Gems. In return for a free copy of your book, they post honest reviews.

As a semi-retired journalist, I have always kept a presence on Facebook through a page. I also have a website. But I resisted starting a review team for a long time. There's nothing as demoralizing as putting together a fan group and there's maybe two or three fans in it.

So what I did in those early days was to bribe my husband and a few friends to join my ARC team so that there would be some people. After some of my overseas trips, I also posted photos exclusively on my review group, which accounted for a few sign-ups.

I got a majority of the sign-ups by asking for ARC readers on my newsletter (which I will talk about in a minute). I just said I have openings on my ARC team if anyone was interested. I used to give out my ARCs to anyone that breathed, but I have since learned that I lost a lot of potential buyers that way, not to mention I didn't get the reviews that I wanted.

So now on my ARC team, about a week before launch date, I post a google doc and have ARC readers "apply" for each book. This way, they can stay on my ARC team without the pressure of reviewing every single book that I post. I ask about five days before I want the reviews, mostly because I have already uploaded my book and it's on three-day lockout in pre-order so I cannot tweak it anymore. I then email those who want my book with a Bookfunnel link. I use the paid subscription on Bookfunnel so that I could gather emails for my newsletter.

I have found that doing it as above, I get a better review rate than when I just put it out there shotgun-style hoping for reviewers. I suspect those who have to go through hoops also take their role a bit more seriously and feel guilty if they don't do as they promise.

Other ways you can use and activate your ARC team:

- Ask them for feedback on your covers.
- Poll them on which plot to do next on your series.
- Do cover reveals there first, so there is added value to their membership.

- Celebrate milestones, or when you finish books, launch a book, get a new cover.
- Share your process either through a short group post or a link to your blog.
- Get to know them by polling them on their reader preferences.
- Recognize that they are most likely reading for other authors, too. Be appreciative of what they are able to do for you. Don't be a nag. No one wants to be around one. Don't issue ultimatums of when they need to get a review back to you. They are doing you a favor by taking the time to read your book. If not now, then later.

***

How to give out review copies of your book

Our main goal as authors of course, is to sell books. However, giving out books for free can be beneficial too, for the following reasons. 1) A free day could mean paid downloads the next day, 2) you want someone to get a copy of your book in advance (ARC) and 3) you want to include your book in a joint promo with other authors through websites like Bookfunnel.

Personally, I have liked the easy interface on Bookunnel. I can upload three formats for my book—mobi (the file format for Amazon), epub and PDF—and my readers could choose whichever format they want. It makes giving out the books seem more professional, and cuts down on the time to attach the big book files onto an email.

***

How to optimize your Bookfunnel experience

Once you have a BF account, you can upload a newsletter magnet. Usually, it is a short book that is a good example of your writing. At the back of this magnet, you can invite a reader to try your series or whichever book you wish to push.

As with anything in publishing, you have one chance to make a good impression. Pay for a professional cover design that meets genre expectations. On these joint promos, your book is competing for attention with others'.

NOTES

Chapter 24: Do Newsletter Swaps

Here is a super-effective marketing tool that is absolutely free: newsletter swaps with other authors. This is why starting a newsletter is such a good idea.

I resisted starting a newsletter email for the longest time. For one, I didn't like getting them myself. I am subscribed to dozens of them, all trying to get me to click in my inbox all day. I also was intimidated by how techie it sounded.

Turns out my fears were unfounded. After the initial setup, it was a breeze. I use Mailerlite and I love it.

You will start out small, at first. I found my first subscribers at community events. I put out a gift card and had people give me their email addresses on their entry.

Put your newsletter sign-up in the front and back of your books. But I wanted to do some newsletter swaps with other authors so I bit the bullet, paid my Mailerlite fee, and started my weekly newsletter.

Publishing a newsletter has been a game changer for me. Apart from the obvious, which was to be able to collect the emails of potential readers and contact them whenever I have a new release, I had a tool I could use to get in front of the email lists of other authors.

Swap with authors who write in similar genres. For example, if you write clean romance, swap with those who write clean romance. You don't want to alienate your subscribers if they expect a certain heat level from you and your books.

Build your newsletter by writing a newsletter magnet. It can be a short story of 5k to 30k words. Or an excerpt of the first book in your series.

Don't worry that you have a small number of subscribers. For a long time, I had thirty subscribers. After a couple of group promos through Bookfunnel, I ended up with over 1,000 subscribers. It continues to grow as I increase my backlist.

To arrange swaps, go to Facebook author groups and network. Share a bit about your book so they know what you want them to feature. List your open dates. I put my newsletter out on Tuesdays, but you can pick whichever date works for you. Over time, I have learned to ask for the author's pen name and book title so I am not scrambling for that information at the last minute. I plug in that info in my calendar.

Once I am done sending out a newsletter with their book, I comment with a link to my newsletter tagging and thanking that author.

NOTES

Chapter 25: Create a positive social media presence

I get that a majority of authors are introverted. It's hard to put yourself out there. Most of us would rather stay inside, shut the door and be a hermit. Some authors have the belief that their readers don't care about their personal life, and would rather just hear about the next book.

That's fine, I suppose.

Frankly, to me, readers are just...people. Brilliant, I know. Just like you and me, people crave to connect. We want to feel valued. We like it when people are interested in us. There are millions of authors on the planet. Why not be that author who connects with others?

Perhaps because of my journalist background, my life has been an open book since I started writing articles and essays in my teens. I bet if you google my name you will read about that time when I joined a rock band as a thirty-something mom. Or that time when I learned how to ride a bicycle in Florida...in my twenties.

Because I am so candid in sharing my photos, writings, and experiences, many people "like" my posts. I am constantly building a platform where, occasionally, I will mention that I have a new book.

That said, there is a fine line between sharing and over-sharing. You don't want to spam people about your book. That's obnoxious and could backfire by people unfollowing you on social media.

Bottom line: whether or not you like social media, it is a great way to get yourself and your books in front of a large group of potential buyers.

TAKEAWAYS

- Be yourself on social media. Be real. Share personal stuff as you are comfortable.

- Be sincere.

- Stay positive. People like happy people. Sure, bad things happen, but look around and you will see that blessings outweigh the negatives.

- Post on your author page regularly. You can copy that same content and put it on your blog. You are then doubling the reach of your efforts while making your blog searchable.

- Use your personal and author page cover as your book billboard. Highlight a series or new release on it. Make sure your graphics show up good on a phone screen.

NOTES

Chapter 26: Run ads or hire them out

Sustaining your sales simply by producing a new book is not realistic. In this ever-changing landscape, experts predict that Amazon Marketing Services (AMS) and Facebook ads will provide authors with the maximum exposure.

AMS ads are those ads that you see under book products on your Amazon page. Facebook ads look like posts, except they say "Sponsored" above them. Books have been written about these topics, so I will not cover them here extensively, but I did want to share my experience of when I hired someone to start AMS ads for me.

In November, in the middle of my Rapid Release, I hired an AMS manager. I had never done this before—running an ad on Amazon and hiring a PA—and she basically hit the ground running. She has a business degree, had taken bestselling author Elana Johnson's AMS class and manages ads for her author daughter.

For $60 she advertised for me for a month. I gave her manager access to my KDP account and 150-character ad copy. Her advice was to make the copy intriguing but not give away the plot and to make sure my cover was a good thumbnail. She had seen my billionaire series and said it looked good.

To start with, she searched and plugged in the keywords I needed. Every week, we assessed how the ads were going. She set my budget for $2 a day. It's highly competitive, and we were aiming for 45-85 cents a click.

Midway through, I noticed that some sponsored books were racy, so she searched some impressions and paused keywords that may have been doing that.

She said, "Things look good Jewel. You have good click through rate and I adjusted some keywords and hope to get more impressions with the clean romance keywords."

She said about a third of the way, "Checked your ad, it's doing great, 2 sales, 70 clicks at an average of .47 per click. I would be happy with 56 clicks so it's doing better than our goal."

I am glad one of us understood the significance of this because I didn't but I did a happy dance anyway.

Ultimately, I spent about $60 on ads, 4 sales with 1k impressions, and possibly some KU exposure.

Although I was getting clicks, I wasn't getting a big bump in sales like I was hoping for, so we paused the ads and I will probably take this up again next year.

She did advise that maybe I could try putting what I would spend otherwise on ads and their management on paid newsletters, that they have better sell-through, so I will have to give that a try in the coming year. She suggested places like Robin

Reads where you could do well with free and 99 cent books for $40 each ad.

Overall, I am glad I tried AMS ads. It was sure nice to hire it out to someone who knew what they were doing, could set it up for me and give me perspective on my stats. Since I was rapid releasing, it was such a relief to turn over the supervision of the ads to someone else, let alone starting it.

For more information on AMS ads, I recommend Brian Meeks' how-to book, *Mastering Amazon Ads*.

NOTES

Chapter 27: Record everything and repeat

One of the habits ingrained in me as a journalist over the last three decades is to record everything. When I experience something significant, when I travel somewhere, when I do something for the first time, I usually process it all by recording it, usually on my blog or Facebook author page.

Similarly, when I started rapid releasing, I wrote often about my publishing journey. Milestones. Interesting trends. Figures. Thanks to this, I have data and memories at my disposal. I am also kind of verbose in my answers on Facebook. So sometimes, I will write a response to someone's question about rapid releasing or billionaire romances, and I would copy that into a blog post.

As you embark on this journey of rapid releasing, write things down. Your impressions. Your fears. Your accomplishments. Take screenshots of your sales. You will be glad you did. Because as you look back, you will know what worked, what didn't. You will remember the bittersweet moments that made up your author journey.

NOTES

Chapter 28: Costs & Revenues of Rapid Release

I will be completely transparent here so you can make the decision for yourself if the cost vs. revenue of Rapid Releasing is for you. Book Report is great, by the way, to distill this information. Your mileage may vary, but it is possible to make a profit from the get-go.

Here are my costs and revenue since Rapid Releasing. I did not spend any money on advertising, well, except for that $120 in November, because I haven't had time to tackle that yet. For formatting, I format my book on Word and then upload it on Draft2Digital for free, which saved me money.

Based on my author friends' experiences, advertising can scale up an author's income. I enrolled in an advertising course and that is the next thing I want to learn.

Costs per book
E-book cover with series discount	$95
Formatting (self-format)	$0
Advertising ($120 divided by 6)	$20

Editing (Average of 2 editors)	<u>$500</u>
Total Cost per book	$595
Total Cost for series so far	$3,690

Revenue (Aug 20, 2018 to Jan 10, 2019)

Her Billionaire Bodyguard	
$3,146.28	
Her Billionaire Prince	
$1,004.88	
Her Billionaire Cowboy	$500.24
Her Billionaire Santa	$356.15
Her Billionaire Spy	$296.95
A Cowboy for Christmas (new series)	$985.78
My backlist of 10 other books	<u>$177.77</u>
Total Revenue	
$6,468.06	
Revenue minus Costs	
$2778.06	

It's worth noting that a majority of my revenue came from enrolling my books in Kindle Unlimited. KU is a program on Amazon where readers can borrow up to a certain number of titles. An author gets paid per page read.

NOTES

Chapter 29: My Rapid Release Timeline

It is January 2019 and I have been publishing a 50k-word book a month since August 2018. Some people publish as frequently as weekly. I like a month between books so that the new release can shine, have a full month of newsletter swaps, and I can savor the milestone. My review team can also keep up with this schedule better.

My schedule goes as follows: one to two weeks to write the draft, one week to betas and editor I've pre-arranged, one week on revisions. All four but the first were on pre-order.

As I have mentioned earlier, pre-orders can be very stressful. I once missed a deadline because I forgot that the deadline was Greenwich Mean Time. Fortunately, the nice folks at Amazon pushed the correct file to my readers. On Christmas Day. If that isn't customer service, I don't know what is.

Pre-orders are great because I can put a link to my next book with every release. For my billionaire series, I contracted five covers in advance so that I could put the next cover in the back of each release. I've sold anywhere from 15 to 70 pre-orders per book.

When I wrote a 12k word novella, I finished it in two days, had betas read it, and had it up as a newsletter magnet a week later. I loved how quick having a fully-formed story was and would love to do more novellas, but for now I will focus on the 50k — so I can price it higher, for the page reads, and so I could develop more of a romance / story arc.

Before this year, it took me months to publish. The pre-orders have been a good motivator to publish on a schedule but I will admit, balance has been lacking so I hope to stockpile drafts ahead of time so my months aren't such a treadmill.

NOTES

Chapter 30: How to Write a Clean Billionaire Romance

From a blog post I wrote on September 18, 2018:

I have been published since 2014, but I didn't encounter as much commercial success until I wrote in a hot-selling genre this summer: clean billionaire romance.

I have been busy writing, editing and publishing, and haven't even delved into paid advertising or promos (except for that one month), and yet my first book, *Her Billionaire Bodyguard*, has stayed in the top 100 paid in its categories and have placed as low as the hundreds in overall paid Amazon ranking (the lower the number, the better). I have spread the word mainly through newsletter swaps and social media.

Here are some tips for those aspiring to write clean billionaire romances:

- **Think series.** Billionaire romance readers are voracious readers. Once they discover an author they enjoy, they will most likely buy your next book. How to tie in each title? Here are some possible tie-ins: geography, setting, trope (fake marriage, etc.). In my series *Her Billionaire CEO*, my billionaires are all CEOs of their respective companies. Scour Amazon's bestselling series for ideas.

- **Start the series off with a great book that meets genre expectations.** Make no mistake, there is some tough competition out there, not just in this genre, but overall. Many readers can tell the difference between a well-executed versus a shoddy book. Good professional editing costs a lot, but this is not the area to skimp. $200 on the low end and $600 on the high end for a 50k word novel, but it will pay off when your reader decides to buy the next book.

- **Publish as quickly as you can to keep your readers' interest.** I used to think I couldn't do it, too. It took me years to produce my first novel. With a hot genre like billionaire romance, however, it helps to do a rapid release. I wrote *Her Billionaire Bodyguard* in five days. (Which is crazy and I haven't replicated it since, but it can be done!) That said, be realistic. Don't try to put out a book a month during a busy time in your life. But it is doable. Set a goal and go for it.

- **Keep your launches consistent.** My plan was to produce one book a month August to

Christmas. So far so good. It's scary but it's also been a good motivator to have my deadlines. I know other authors who publish more frequently. Do what works for you. One important note: a rapid release series does cost money between covers and editing. You will want to save up and invest in it.

- **Get a professional cover.** A guy on the cover or a couple? Either way, hire a cover artist so that your cover sells your book. Some cover designers charge as little as $50. I know some people use Fiverr, but unless you get a Fiverr artist highly recommended, it's hit and miss. I've hired a couple and have been underwhelmed with results. If you prefer to make your cover, study bestselling books in the genre for inspiration.

- **Fulfill genre expectations.** Read a lot of billionaire and regular romances. Subscribe to Kindle Unlimited and read highly rated books. Pay attention to the opening hook, kissing scenes, romantic conflict, the black moment, and the resolution. Notice what makes you swoon as a reader. After a while, you will see a pattern that can help you in your storytelling. My editor gave me this great advice: put in feels, then add more feels.

- **Dream big.** Billionaires live larger-than-life and need bombastic stories. Most of them have staff like bodyguards, personal assistants, chefs, chauffeurs. Google billionaire lifestyles and be prepared to have your jaw drop. Then write the fun details into your story.

- **Get over your money hang-ups.** If you've ever wanted to spend money you don't have, write in this genre. You can own luxury cars, go on fantasy dates, and buy expensive dresses...without whipping out your credit card. Readers want to escape. Give them what they want, and they will love you. I think that's one of the draws to the megahit movie *Crazy Rich Asians*. A helicopter trip to a tropical river? Check. Fireworks at your engagement party? Check. Lavish wedding with water flowing into the aisles? Check. Shopping spree for wedding guests? Check.

- **Keep it clean.** Clean billionaire romance readers prefer no explicit sex, no sex before marriage, mild to no cursing, and no graphic violence. You have the right to include whatever you want in your book, but if you want to fit in to "clean and wholesome," fulfilling the guidelines above will make you a reader favorite. The surest way to turn off a reader is to not fulfill a promise. If you claim that your book is clean, be sure to deliver.

- **Research, then have fun making it up.** "Write what you know" is a famous saying. Well, how do you write about being a billionaire when you are in reality strapped for money? Google a setting and the lifestyle, then just use your imagination. Real billionaires are too busy making money; no one is going to call you out on the accuracy of your plot line.

- That said, **write a believable story.** How do you police this? Get beta readers who read or write in the genre and listen when they say, "This isn't believable..." Don't panic if they do. Just figure out a way to make it believable. Sometimes it takes just a sentence or two of explanation.

- **Give your billionaire a conscience.** No one likes an arrogant wealthy person. Consider giving your billionaire philanthropic tendencies. Have them start a foundation. Have them attend charity events and donate.

- **If you do start out your billionaire as a jerk, redeem them at the end of your book.** They can start out a "bad boy" but if you give him a story arc where he changes for good, that will endear him (and you) to your reader.

- **Pair your billionaire romance with trope favorites such as prince or cowboy.** This will make your book more appealing to a wider swath of readers. Her Billionaire Bodyguard uses the– surprise! — bodyguard trope. A reader told me they loved my book and this was the first bodyguard book they'd read. I get that. There aren't many clean bodyguard books out there. That's what's fun about giving readers clean options. See what billionaire romances are selling and put a clean spin to it.

- **Network with other clean billionaire romance authors.** Or other clean romance authors. Swapping newsletters has been one of the most effective ways my book has gained traction in the market.

- **Use the word billionaire in the title.** Or in the series title or description. That helps with discoverability.

- **Embrace the genre wholeheartedly.** You want to write a romance, so why not a billionaire one, a genre that is selling? Tweak a story idea and add a few zeroes to a character's net worth. Write great books.

Some people might never pick up a clean billionaire romance for whatever reason. And that's fine. There's plenty enough who do.

NOTES

Chapter 31: Case Study: Her Billionaire Bodyguard

Her Billionaire Bodyguard was the first in my clean billionaire romance series *Her Billionaire CEO*. When I launched on my 46th birthday on August 24, 2018, I had no fanbase for this series. I had thirty subscribers in my brand spanking new newsletter. But it has by far been the most profitable launch I have ever had.

In its first 30 days alone, I made back over four times what I had spent on the book—$2,210.59. I have not replicated it yet, although I am excited at its potential. This strong first book has been funneling readers into the rest of my series. I have plans for a total of at least nine books in *Her Billionaire CEO*.

I chalk this up to the following factors:

- A professional cover. I was going to do it myself, but when I asked for feedback on the usual "billionaire in a suit on the front of a billionaire romance," my author friends candidly told me it was a fail. So, I went back to the drawing board and picked a cute couple, then changed the title from My

Billionaire Bodyguard to Her Billionaire Bodyguard. Someone said the white background was too bland, so I added a pink and purple concert background. It looked photoshopped, though. So finally, I commissioned a professional cover artist to do it for me. She not only made it look natural, she branded the series with the title and logo and overall look. It was the best $100 I have spent.

- Unique but still appealing take on the billionaire cover. I took a chance and put a couple on my cover, which I believe makes my series stand out, but not too much that billionaire romance readers would avoid it.

- A professional editor. I paid $500 for a developmental editor to help me with the book. As it was a bodyguard trope, I picked an editor who not only writes popular romance novels but also is a firefighter for his day job. I swallowed painfully as I forked out the money, but luckily, I made my money back and some. The great reviews have been good not just for that book, but for the rest of the series and my backlist.

- A hot genre. Clean Billionaire romance sells itself without much effort. Remember, I made this profit only by swapping with other authors for newsletter spots.

- Hot tropes. Bodyguard and second chance romance tropes helped draw readers.

- Fabulous beta readers. I lucked out. I had beta read for a couple of established authors in the romance genre and they made invaluable suggestions to my manuscript. I learned a lot from them about how much to push and pull in a romance. How much I should let the characters touch or not.

- Newsletter swaps with other authors of clean romance.

- Endorsement of a popular publisher/ author who read it on her sick day and gushed about it to her newsletter list of over ten thousand. After her boost, I nearly made it to #1 in Clean & Wholesome. It was a fun ride.

- The promise of an exciting series. As soon as I launched this book, I had put the next one up for pre-order. Having the two books visually on my page probably drummed up excitement for the rest of the series. Later, I put up most of my covers so that the series could catch a potential reader's eye.

- Selling it at 99 cents very well could have helped, although as you will see in the next chapter, that doesn't necessarily work for all books.

- Luck and divine intervention. No doubt.

***

Launching *Her Billionaire Bodyguard*

On August 28, 2018, I shared launch stats of *Her Billionaire Bodyguard* in a Facebook post.

***

My little book that could, *Her Billionaire Bodyguard*, ended today with a rank of #20 Clean & Wholesome, #51 Inspirational, #78 Billionaires, #1486 overall. UPDATE: On 8/31 it reached #8 Clean & Wholesome, #19 Inspirational, #36 Billionaires and #685 overall. Thanks to all my newsletter (NL) swappers!!!!

I haven't paid for any advertising (I'm not that organized yet). It's all been NL swaps (which I arranged three weeks ahead of time) and social media posts/shares. My guess is, writing to market in a popular genre, 99 cent price, pro editing & cover, awesome betas and good reviews all helped, too. Here's how my launch has played out, if you're interested:

8/21 Uploaded e-book in anticipation of 8/24 official launch. Set the price to 99 cents as a series intro promo. Enrolled in KU.

8/22 #82,049 Amazon rank

8/22 #118,499. 285 page reads

8/23 #52,519. Bought my own copy. Asked my ARC team to post reviews. (I had given out ARCs a week before launch.)

8/24 Posted my book's birthday (and mine) on my timeline, Clean Indie Reads, Breaking Amazon Top 100, Sweet Bookaholic Readers. Asked for FB & Twitter shares. By 12:32 pm #26,835. I had requested Amazon to link this book to book 2 of the series, which is on pre-order, and they did. I dropped the price of Book 2 to 2.99. By 4:50 pm #16,294, sold 15 books, have three reviews. Sold some pre-orders of Book 2. By 11:11 pm #12,264

8/25 #14,767, 5 5-star reviews. Ended day with #13,477

8/27 #23,257, 1500 page reads. Posted link on Clean Billionaire Romance. Got my paperback proof & posted pic on Instagram, my FB timeline and The Writing Gals. Ended with #13,409. By 10:30 pm, over 2k page reads.

8/28 12:20 p.m. #4,944 paid overall. #82 in Clean & Wholesome. 2:20 p.m. #2,001 overall. #31 C&W. 5:20 p.m. #25 C&W, #88 Billionaires, #1830 overall. By day's end #20 C&W, #49 Inspirational, #78 Billionaires, #1486 overall.

UPDATE: 8/31 #8 C&W, #19 Inspirational, #36 Billionaires. #685 overall.

NOTES

Chapter 32: Case Study: A Cowboy for Christmas

Some of my fellow authors speculated this past Christmas that 99-cent Christmas books were distracting from full-price books. Some authors also wondered whether to sell Christmas books at full-price or 99 cents.

I released two Christmas books, both sweet romance. *Her Billionaire Santa* (HBS, 4th in a series) at 99 cents on 11/24/18 and *A Cowboy for Christmas* (ACFC, 1st in a series) at 2.99 on 12/14/18. They both run 50k words.

A Cowboy for Christmas was a manuscript I had completed in NaNoWriMo 2017, unearthed and decided to publish as the start of a series in the middle of my Her Billionaire CEO series.

No ads, just newsletter swaps with authors in a similar genre and shares on clean read and western romance groups. I also participated in two Christmas FB events.

ACFC total revenue $852.50, 160 sales, 105,758 pages read

Highest rank: #1413

HBS total revenue $315.06, 143 sales, 39,379 pages read

Highest rank: #4093

My takeaways:

- If you are writing in a strong genre, like cowboy romance, keeping your book at full price is a good move.

- Put out a good product and people will buy it at full price.

- Don't undervalue your work. Don't be afraid to charge full price. That said, there may be some marketing value to making your book free for a day. Many authors report good sales once the book is more visible due to a higher ranking, which leads to substantial sales.

- Professional covers that hit genre expectations make a huge difference in sales. ACFC was my highest selling book in December and it only sold for the last two weeks of the month. I got a huge sales spike when I released ACFC. I attribute that a lot to the cover.

- Christmas Day sales are strong. They account for the biggest spike in my

December sales. I did also release my fifth book in my billionaire series on 12/24 so that might have helped all around.

- For ACFC, I did not do a pre-order, just did an FB cover reveal. Pre-orders are great for series but not necessary for strong sales.

- Selling at 99 cents does not necessarily boost your rank over a $2.99 book. ACFC highest rank #1413. HBS highest rank #4093.

- I have over 1k on my NL list. Every time I shared about either books in a casual, non-spammy way, I got spikes in sales. NLs are worth it.

- If you can write a Christmas book, it is a great boost for your series. Christmas books sell.

- Christmas books are a joy to write. These two books were my first in the genre, and if I had more time, I would have put out yet another one.

In January 2019, I am starting a series of newsletter swaps this month for ACFC. I pre-arranged them in early December. I am hoping that will keep my sales going. I also plan to write a sequel soon to take advantage of interest in that first book.

NOTES

Chapter 33: Pros & Cons of Rapid Releasing

I won't lie.

Rapid Releasing has been one of the most challenging, physically and mentally demanding work that I have ever done in my life. During drafting and revising weeks, I am usually up at the crack of dawn trying to get a head start on my wordcount and often go to bed late. The good thing is it's intense for a bit, and then I can relax on the off-times. And the work is flexible.

The unforgiving drumbeat of pre-orders (if you choose to do this) marches on despite holidays, birthdays, kids being home from college, a trip to Mexico the week your pre-order is due or anything else going on in your life.

It can take a toll on your health with all that sitting for long hours. Dictation is a viable alternative to the keyboard.

Unless you plan ahead and pile up manuscripts (which I strongly recommend), you will not have time for much else in your life.

Rapid Releasing is doable, but you have to strive constantly to maintain balance in your life.

***

There are benefits of course.

As a storyteller, you will get stronger as you craft story after story in such a short amount of time. Today I am quicker to plot and I can write a hook-opening with minimal thought.

You can earn money fast. Each new release in a series will sell your backlist. You will be able to invest money from book sales into your publishing business.

Producing books quickly will boost your confidence as an author.

Finally, unless you advertise heavily, it's easier to keep your readers' interest in future books in your series if you can publish every month or two.

With some advance planning, Rapid Releasing can be an exciting, rewarding and exhilarating experience.

NOTES

Chapter 34: Q&A with bestselling author Bree Livingston

Bree Livingston is the pen name of an author who started rapid releasing on March 10, 2018. She made over $2k that month. From March to December of 2018, she grossed $87k. She has 14 published books in the clean & wholesome romance genre. Visit her at www.breelivwrites.allauthor.com

Q. **Why did you choose a pen name and how do you think you managed to break out without an established readership?**

A. I'd published under a different name and since I was publishing WTM (written to market) I wanted a clean start. (I was still writing clean, just Christian.)

To make sure that the WTM name didn't have ties to other genres.

It's funny. I chose Bree Livingston by going to a font website and finding a name that would look pretty all scrolled out.

As for how I broke out?

That I don't know. That first story struck a chord with readers. I posted in the NL swap group, and next thing I knew my book was going out in a ton of NL's.

I haven't done NL builders very much. I don't like them. I did do one and it resulted in roughly 200 people joining my NL, but my open rate went down. I have my NL in the back of my book and that's how people join.

Honestly, and for people who aren't believers...this next statement won't make any sense. God blessed me.

Q. **I noticed your God-centered posts and I think that is so cool. Remind me what your first book was.**

A. Her Pretend Billionaire Boyfriend.

Q. **What is your writing background?**

A. HAHAHA. Um, I have an accounting degree?

Q. **No way. Of course, publishing is a business. How did you segue into writing?**

A. Oh, about ten years ago or maybe longer, I got up in the middle of the night and wrote something. I was told I was a good story teller. Over the next decade I wrote a book, and then published it in 2016.

I wrote three more before the end of that year and published two of them.

Q. I remember when you started writing your billionaire books, you already had two or three before you started publishing. Is that right?

A. Yes. At least three done before I started publishing.

Q. How did you decide what kind of series to write? Why billionaires?

A. Actually, I spoke to (bestselling author) Victorine Lieske and she encouraged me to write to market and that was billionaires.

Q. Describe your writing process for that first breakout book.

A. Oh boy.
I needed a way to keep my hero and heroine together, a boat seemed a good way to do that, and it went from there. It took me about 10 days to write that one.

Q. Wow. Nice. 10 days. How did the revision process go? Any tips there? Because for me, that is the hardest thing.

A. Uh, that first book was my hardest, but mostly it was making my heroine less like myself and not a doormat. Christina (my editor) griped at me about that. Once I had that done, it was good to go.

I learned a lot last year. When I'm writing, I've got Christina in my head asking me questions.

Q. **Ha, ha, funny. Just as we are talking here, Christina is messaging me about my book that is due on pre-order tomorrow. Sorry to be so blunt, but can I ask you how much money you have made by rapid releasing?**

A. Uh, I made 87k last year in comparison to 2017 which netted me a whopping $280 (roughly).

Q. **Wow! So is that after expenses? And over how many books, what length, etc.**

A. That's before expenses. I had losses from January, February, and March that ate into what I made. So, my after expenses was 44k.

Q. **Still. That's awesome.**

A. Yeah. I was very happy with it.

Q. **Do you feel that there is a magic number to a series? Before you and the readers are bored? I noticed you branched out to bride romances. Is that doing as well as billionaires?**

A. Magic number? No, not really. I was doing fiver per series until my readers gave me the thumbs up for publishing my sixth billionaire book. It was one I'd written and set aside thinking I'd never publish it. So, it's been well received.

I don't think readers get as bored as we think. A good story is a good story. Whether it's the first book or the fiftieth.

Billionaire is still rocking it. I did decent with the fake marriage, but the billionaire one still rocks it. That sixth billionaire book had all of $69 in paid promo and it got to less than 500 in Amazon paid. Plus, not to toot my own horn, but I have a following now. I only have an ARC team of 24. My first book, Pretend, I sent out all of 4 ARCs.

Q. **Let's talk stats for a minute. NL subscribers? Books total? ARC team?**

A. I have 391 NL subscribers now. Started with 13 and several were fellow authors. I have 14 published books. And 24 total on my ARC team. I like to keep my ARC team small. I think it makes them feel special and more likely to leave a review.

Q. **Do you write your books month to month? Or do you stockpile?**

A. I'm trying to get ahead and stockpile but I'm month to month as we speak. I hope to fix that in the coming month.

Q. Ha ha, I hear you. Do you do pre-orders?

A. Nope. I don't do those with my WTM. I do the slow release method.

Q. I probably shouldn't either. I just like having links to share.

A. I can see the advantage. I'm just set in my ways. Lol

Q. Tips to avoid losses? Biggest takeaway?

A. Tell a good story and your readers will be very forgiving. Don't throw money at promo sites known to not work.

Biggest takeaway? Backlist, backlist, backlist.

NOTES

Chapter 35: Other Authors, on Rapid Releasing

On August 13, 2018, I was on the verge of my first Rapid Release of a clean billionaire romance series. In an indie author's Facebook group, I lamented that rapid releasing felt like gambling so much money.

I wrote, "I know I have to just bite the bullet and have faith, but it's unnerving. Anyone want to hold my hand so to speak? Or give me some tough love. Either way."

Here is the advice that several awesome authors gave me.

Brian Meeks: $600.00 is VERY little to spend on publishing a book and you have your whole life to earn it back. Not that I think it will take that long, but don't worry about whether you'll be profitable...you will be.

Bree Livingston: I publish every thirty days. With that in mind, I write the story, send it to my editor, then my proofer, get my cover done, and then publish. Typically, as soon as I have one story written, I start on the next so that once the book that's currently with my editor is done, I can send the next. So, say if I plan to publish in March, I'll have the story to my editor by February.

It can burn you out because the schedule you're on is tight. You have to have that next story written so your editor has time to work on it. If you don't have some focus to get that word count done, it can get hairy trying to get that story done so that you can publish on time.

For me, if I'm struggling with a story, I'll run through my trope lists, looking for inspiration. I'll even go to my critique group with something and have them help me brainstorm. There are times I've gone to my editor for help. You take it where you can get it. You never know what suggestion will spark something.

The bottom like to my process is getting words on the page. You can't publish what you haven't written.

Audrey Rich: You'll recover your investment and be able to fund future books.

Lacy Andersen: I'm in the midst of my second rapid release of three books. It's a great way to gain momentum and capture your audience read through. I think most of our clients have limited patience to wait for the next in a series, so why not try to make it easy on them? And from everything I've researched and learned about making money indie publishing, most authors don't start making serious money until they have a series out.

I work a part-time job on the side to help recoup the costs for my family until the books start making money.

Lucy Roberts: From beginning to end (including promotion) I spend $431.00 and I thankfully make that back with preorders so I come out of the starting gate in the green. I do 20 to 30k novellas and full length. I publish every three weeks on the dot.

Kristen Iten: Just gotta keep the faith and forge ahead. We've got a good product and there is a market.

Chandelle LaVaun: I did the same thing this year, scrambling to finish book 5 as we speak. The money part hurts, especially at first, but I had a waitress job that helped me pay the bills. I'd pick up an extra shift or two if I was coming up short. But then you start making money back so that helps!! Have some faith and plow forward!!

Yumoyori Wilson: DO IT :D I've got 13 left to go this year, so I feel you on the investments (I bought most of my covers ahead of time so that hit my pocket) but it's worth it :D. Just make sure you space it out and see if doing one month between each book is worth it or doing two months, etc.

Angel Lawson: If you're considering this a business you have to invest in it. I know this is a hard step but it's so important. The good news is by book three you'll have some $$ coming in and hopefully it will just keep going up!

Brittney Mulliner: I made my own covers for my hockey releases. I doubt I could have done them rapid release without doing that.

Iris Kelly: I would just recommend - even though you've already made that big investment, don't skimp on ads, even though it means more expense. You want to give your series the best chance of being seen. AMS seems to be the easiest and most effective.

Julia Keanini: I've done nine rapid release books, but I'm so tired now I can't remember the pros and cons. ;) But in all seriousness I think it is an amazing marketing tactic. I've done most of mine with preorders but I think I'm going to switch my tactic this year. I plan on releasing 13 books in 2019 so every book will be a part of some kind of rapid release system. Pre-orders seemed to be losing steam for me at the end of 2018.

NOTES

Chapter 36: To Sum Up

Choose a popular genre.
Recognize trends.
Embrace the trend positively.
Write what you love and tweak it to what is trending.

Think series.
Plan a series around similar tropes.
Link standalone books into series.
Aim for at least three in a series.

Use catchy book ideas and titles.
Write the blurb and outline first.

Mock-up the cover as you write.
Hire a cover artist.
Commission series covers at once.

Write your first draft fast.
Prepare to write fast.
Write in Sprints.

Believe that you can.
Enroll your book as a pre-order.
Keep on moving.

You're not writing the Great American Novel.
Write through the dreaded middle slump.

Pay for professional editing.
Utilize beta readers.
Format your book for free.

Form an ARC review team.
Do newsletter swaps.
Create a positive social media presence.
Run AMS ads or hire them out.
Record everything and repeat.

·

NOTES

Chapter 37: Parting Thoughts

On Facebook, an author asked what the publishing trend will be. Here was my prediction and advice to authors.

Billionaires will remain hot. Regency will continue to have timeless appeal. Cowboys will always be strong. Royals will stay fascinating.

Produce good books and you will do well regardless of the trend. But if you can match up your passions with the tropes above, you will most likely do great.

Popular tropes are not a sure thing, but it's close to a sure thing. You can even capitalize on your existing fan base and meld that with the popular books. The only way you will know is if you try it.

Whatever you do, jump in with both feet.

***

Best of luck to you! Let me know how you do or if you have any questions by contacting me at **www.jewelallen.com.** To check out my rapid release series, look up Jewel Allen on Amazon.

Lastly, if you enjoyed this book, could you please review it online? Thank you!

NOTES

About the Author

Jewel Allen is an award-winning journalist, author and ghostwriter who grew up in the Philippines and now lives in Utah. She has a bachelor's degree in English from Utah State University. She loves to visit interesting places in the world and spin stories about them.

Connect with Jewel: **www.jewelallen.com**

CPSIA information can be obtained
at www.ICGtesting.com
Printed in the USA
LVHW090211060619
620349LV00001B/5/P